Advent
Daily Christmas Devotionals

Paul D Grodell III

DEDICATION

To Bethany, Paul David, & Novella

May the God of hope fill you with all joy and peace in believing,
so that by the power of the Holy Spirit you may abound in hope.
Romans 15:13

CONTENTS

WEEK THREE

WEEK FOUR

INTRODUCTION

I grew up in a Jesus-loving, faith-filled family. Both of my parents modeled how to love God and how to serve His church. The way they lived, and still live to this day, has proven to be one of the greatest treasures in my life.

Growing up in that environment produced a healthy respect in me for the importance of Christmas. Sure, as a kid, I looked forward to it for the presents, sweets, and the sound of shredding gift wrap. But those weren't the only reasons.

I was taught the story of the first Christmas from a young age. Every year my parents took time to explain to me the importance of Christ's birth and how it changed the paradigm for humanity's relationship to and with God.

Every year I looked forward to celebrating the birth of Jesus, similar to how I looked forward to my friend's birthday parties. At my friend's birthday parties, I knew there would be cake, games, and maybe even a goodie bag to take home. I knew the point of the birthday party was to celebrate my friend, but what I received at the party came in as a close second. I viewed Christmas this same way for most of my adolescence and into my adult years.

Twenty-some years later, I had been in full-time vocational ministry for quite some time. The Christmas season at church meant fifty-to-sixty-hour work weeks, with the weeks leading up to Christmas being even busier. Throw family traditions into the mix, and it led to me being tired and weary of the season I once loved.

The awe and wonder of Christmas had all but vanished from my life, replaced by traditions that had worn thin, familiar songs, and the hustle and bustle of the holidays. Instead of looking forward to Christmas each year, I dreaded it. It was something to grit my way through rather than slow down and celebrate. That is until 2016.

One night a couple of weeks after Thanksgiving, I happened to be looking through my Kindle downloads and discovered an Advent devotional written by Dietrich Bonhoeffer that I had purchased a few years earlier. [1] At the time, I never actually read more than a few pages and had mostly forgotten about it.

Although I saw nothing wrong with my attitude or perspective on Christmas, I felt a heavy conviction to take time each day to read this specific devotional. They weren't very long and were easy to digest, which made my goal of finishing before Christmas attainable.

By the end of that Christmas season, I had felt the underpinnings of the awe and wonder I experienced as a child return. Only now, it was not the celebration of Christ's birth I was looking forward to, but what the birth pointed toward: the return of Christ.

This is the power of Advent made simple: observing Advent creates an expectation of Christ's second coming inside of us. It accomplishes this by meditating on what it was like for Israel before the first arrival of Christ.

Advent is derived from the Latin adventus, which means coming or arrival. It is a translation of the Greek word parousia (παρουσία), which is used twenty-four times in the New Testament, seventeen of which directly refer to the Second Coming of Christ.

This is significant because it connects those who cried out in the Old Testament for the coming of the Messiah to those who cry out now for His return.

---

[1] Bonhoeffer, D., Riess, J., & Dean, O. C., Jr. (2010b). *God Is in the Manger: Reflections on Advent and Christmas* (7/31/10 ed.). Westminster John Knox Press.

Advent is an invitation to imagine yourself as one of God's people before Jesus was born. It's a call to put yourself in another place and time in history so that you may experience afresh the joy and wonder of Christ's birth. Advent is an experience meant to invoke the longing for His second coming and to bolster one's faith, for if Christ came once to this earth, He shall come again.

I have written this devotional so you can spend as little as ten minutes each day observing Advent. I did this intentionally to remove the excuse of busyness being a barrier to entry.

Each devotional has a short Scripture, followed by my meditation on the passage that should only take two to three minutes to read. After which, I invite you to participate in the traditional practice of Lectio Divina for five to seven minutes.

If you are short on time for a particular day, skip over my writing and go straight to the Lectio Divina practice. I am confident that if you follow practice it, Holy Spirit will meet you there.

Observing Advent taught me to slow down during the holidays to intentionally make space to meet God so that He may quicken in me a desire for Christ's return.

I hope the devotionals in this book help you do the same.

HOPE

He who hopes in God trusts God, Whom he never sees, to bring him to the possession of things that are beyond imagination.[1]

Thomas Merton

---

[1] Merton, T. (2016). *No Man Is an Island* (UK ed.). Hachette Australia.

WEEK 1: DAY ONE

May the God of hope (ἐλπίς) fill you with all joy and peace as you trust in him, so that you may overflow with hope by the power of the Holy Spirit. Romans 15:13 [NIV]

***

On this, the first day of Advent, let us turn to hope. For it is hope that sustains our longing during seasons of difficulty in life. This longing is not simple escapism to get us away from the problems we encounter, as those who have not tasted the joys of walking with God may assume.

The longing the Christian experiences is a longing for the fulfillment of the Kingdom of God on earth as it is in heaven. It's a desire to fully experience the goodness of God, to see His creation shed its garments stained by injustice and evil, and obtain the shroud of love and peace.

Without this longing, we fall into the trap of complacency or desperation. Complacency causes us to live detached from the vocation given to us by God. It whispers to us that what we do in this life has no real meaning, and like an earworm, rings incessantly in our mind telling us to choose the path of least resistance, implying the passage of time will change our circumstances.

Desperation, in contrast, causes us to live in a frantic and exasperated state. It tells us that no relief is coming unless we can manufacture salvation with our power. It bids us to act in ways antithetical to citizenship in God's Kingdom.

We become resentful of those who prosper in ways we desire to prosper. We become spiteful toward those who wrong us. We destroy our bodies through the use of outside substances, or we work ourselves to death as we claw toward the relief of the pain that life brings.

The Greek word for hope, used fifty-four times in the New Testament, is elpís. Thayer's Greek Lexicon defines it as "that in which one confides or to which he flees for refuge." This type of hope is the flame that fuels our Christian longing.

Our hope comes to us not from the simple passing of time or from the desperate actions we can muster but from the God of hope.

When the weight of life drenches us to the bone, we can cling to God with confidence, knowing He will lift us. Even when immediate relief seems to be out of reach, we can look to the work of Christ and gain confidence that the Kingdom of God is both here and on its way.

Hope shakes us out of our complacency by calling us to be active participants in God's redemptive work. It inspires us to wake up with a purpose, to put our hands to the work of reconciling the world back to God.

Hope relieves us of our desperation by reminding us that the Babe in the Manger overthrew the world's kingdoms through meekness, humility, and love. We do not have to strive to save ourselves any longer.

Our salvation brought us hope with His first breath and peace with His last.

LECTIO DIVINA

Take a moment to breathe deeply. Close your eyes and invite Holy Spirit to speak to you as you read God's Word. Your invitation can be as simple as, "God, I recognize that in this moment, as in all moments, I am in your presence. Speak for your servant is listening."

READ:

May the God of hope fill you with all joy and peace as you trust in him, so that you may overflow with hope by the power of the Holy Spirit. Romans 15:13 [NIV]

Take a moment to allow the Scripture to sink in. Now, go back and read it two more times. Each time, read slowly and pay special attention to any word or phrase that sticks out to you.

Ask Holy Spirit to reveal to you why (if any) word or phrase stuck out during your reading. Use the space below to journal your thoughts.

_____

_____

_____

_____

_____

_____

_____

_____

WEEK 1: DAY TWO

Therefore the Lord himself will give you a sign: The virgin will conceive and give birth to a son, and will call him Immanuel.
Isaiah 7:14 [NIV]

The virgin will conceive and give birth to a son, and they will call him Immanuel" (which means "God with us).
Matthew 1:23 [NIV]

***

The first Advent candle is often called the Prophecy Candle. It symbolizes the hope Israel had for the coming Messiah. The candle is meant to stand as a light shining in the darkness to symbolize how God's presence in the darkest times.

The story of Israel is filled with many seemingly dark moments. From the failures of its greatest leaders to the terrors of tyrants taking them to hostile lands, the Hebrew Scriptures drip with anticipation for an Anointed One to lead the people back into the presence of God.

It can be hard for those of us who live on this side of the covenant to place ourselves in the desperate state that the people of God lived in before the birth of Christ, particularly those of us who live in Western culture.

Though it can be hard to imagine the desperation for a deliverer one feels when living under generations of foreign rule, all of us can likely recall a time when we felt distant, perhaps even cut off, from God.

I can recall a season in my life when it felt as if God was no nearer to me than the moon. I searched my heart to see if there was any unrepentant sin, disobedience, or bitterness toward God. Each time I searched, I came up empty.

No matter how hard I pressed into the spiritual practices that had sustained and nourished my life, and no matter how long I waited in prayer, no matter how much Scripture I read, in a very real and terrifying sense, I could no longer feel God's presence.

This perceived distance from God would wake me up in the middle of the night. It would pull me out of beautiful moments with my family like a bolt of lightning crashing into a great oak.

Thankfully, God had given me graces through the prior experiences of Him that I had in my youth and on into my adult years. I knew these experiences were true and not mere fits of happiness, and they kept drawing me back to God in prayer. They were the light in the darkness that encouraged me to hold on to hope.

Like Israel, I found solace in the fact that God was with me in past trials, that He was always faithful to carry me to His victory, and that His provision over my life had never failed. It was seeing and remembering the light of God's past faithfulness that carried me through the darkness.

For as St. Francis of Assisi said, "All the darkness in the world cannot extinguish the light of a single candle."

LECTIO DIVINA

Take a moment to breathe deeply. Close your eyes and invite Holy Spirit to speak to you as you read God's Word. Your invitation can be as simple as, "God, I recognize that in this moment, as in all moments, I am in your presence. Speak for your servant is listening."

READ:
Therefore the Lord himself will give you a sign: The virgin will conceive and give birth to a son, and will call him Immanuel. Isaiah 7:14 [NIV]

"The virgin will conceive and give birth to a son, and they will call him Immanuel" (which means "God with us"). Matthew 1:23 [NIV]

Take a moment to allow the Scriptures to sink in. Now, go back and read it two more times. Each time, read slowly and pay special attention to any word or phrase that sticks out to you.

Ask Holy Spirit to reveal to you why (if any) word or phrase stuck out during your reading. Use the space below to journal your thoughts.

_____

_____

_____

_____

_____

_____

_____

17

WEEK 1: DAY THREE

Praise be to the Lord, the God of Israel, because he has come to his people and redeemed them. 69 He has raised up a horn of salvation for us in the house of his servant David 70 (as he said through his holy prophets of long ago), Luke 1:68-70 [NIV]

***

In Psalm 18, David cries out in praise to God for delivering him from the hands of his enemies. David then describes God as "the horn of my salvation."

A horn in the animal kingdom is a sign of strength and dominance. It is used to fight and protect. Often in Scripture, a horn is a literary symbol of salvation meant to represent power and potency.

This is the picture of Messiah given to Zechariah in the temple when he is filled with Holy Spirit to prophesy about Jesus' birth. He says that God has redeemed His people and has raised up "a horn of salvation for us in the house of his servant David."

The name of Jesus is likely one of the most well-known in all of human history, yet many people don't know the etymology of the name. Jesus is a Greek translation of a Hebrew name: Yehoshua, or, as we know the name in English: Joshua.

Joshua was a warrior king in the Hebrew Scriptures. He was a general. A military man. Battle-hardened. He conquered

18

kingdoms. He overthrew armies. He was the man tasked with bringing Israel into the promised land.

And his name meant "Yahweh (God) saves."

When the angel tells Joseph in Matthew 1:21 to "name him Jesus, for he will save his people from their sins," he says that because the name Jesus literally means "God saves."

Believe it or not, many people in Jesus's day looked to Jesus as a type of savior. Over and over again in the New Testament, we see people come to Jesus, hoping He will save them from the oppression of Rome.

This is because the people of God in Jesus's day were looking for another Joshua. They were desperate for a new warrior king to deliver them from their oppressors. Someone to lead them to victory in battle. They wanted to be out from under the tyranny of Rome, so they were looking for a specific type of savior.

They wanted Jesus to be their savior but on their terms. They were interested in a savior coming only so far as the savior could help them in their present circumstance. Much like many of us today.

We measure the effectiveness of Christ's work in our life by what's in our bank account or if our political candidate wins. We measure His effectiveness by what we like or dislike about our life, health, or our happiness.

The truth is that Jesus didn't come to save us from others; He came to save us from ourselves. The angel tells Joseph to name the child Jesus because He will "save his people from **their sins**."

This is the great hope the Christ child brings to humankind.

He has come as the God who saves. He is the horn of our salvation. He is Christ with us.

LECTIO DIVINA

Take a moment to breathe deeply. Close your eyes and invite Holy Spirit to speak to you as you read God's Word. Your invitation can be as simple as, "God, I recognize that in this moment, as in all moments, I am in your presence. Speak for your servant is listening."

READ:
Praise be to the Lord, the God of Israel, because he has come to his people and redeemed them. 69 He has raised up a horn of salvation for us in the house of his servant David 70 (as he said through his holy prophets of long ago), Luke 1:68-70 [NIV]

Take a moment to allow the Scripture to sink in. Now, go back and read it two more times. Each time, read slowly and pay special attention to any word or phrase that sticks out to you.

Ask Holy Spirit to reveal to you why (if any) word or phrase stuck out during your reading. Use the space below to journal your thoughts.

_____

_____

_____

_____

_____

_____

_____

WEEK 1: DAY FOUR

And you, my child, will be called a prophet of the Most High; for you will go on before the Lord to prepare the way for him, 77 to give his people the knowledge of salvation through the forgiveness of their sins, 78 because of the tender mercy of our God, by which the rising sun will come to us from heaven **79 to shine on those living in darkness and in the shadow of death, to guide our feet into the path of peace.** Luke 1:76-79 [NIV]

***

Sit in a dark room long enough, and you'll feel the desperation total darkness brings. You may see or hear things that aren't there. Your heartbeat may quicken as your mind tries to conceive what is lying in the darkness.

Anyone who has been trapped in darkness knows the joy that light brings.

Most of us cannot fathom what it would be like to be trapped in the dark for 400 years. Yet, this is the very metaphor given for Israel (and humanity) before the birth of Christ.

Israel had ignored God's commands. They neglected to honor His word to them. They rejected His prophets. So, God stopped speaking for 400 years.

The desperation for God's presence and word to return to Israel can be witnessed throughout the writings of Haggai, Zechariah, and Malachi. Even though the exiles had returned from captivity, and the Israelites were home once again, home was not the same.

God had not returned with them.

Within this context, Holy Spirit chooses to show up and fill Zechariah, inspiring him to prophecy. When you read his prophecy (Luke 1:68-79), it is brimming with hope and joy.

I love the way Eugene Peterson translates part of Zechariah's prophecy.

"Through the heartfelt mercies of our God, **God's Sunrise will break in upon us,** Shining on those in the darkness, those sitting in the shadow of death, Then showing us the way, one foot at a time, down the path of peace." (Luke 1, Message Version)

When you read that Scripture, you are reading the fulfillment of hundreds of years of prayers. This was the first crack in the breaking clouds. It was a small beam of light piercing through to declare the time of darkness was coming to an end.

The dawn was not far off.

The Light was returning to the earth to remove the shadow of death that loomed over God's people.

The Light was descending to guide humanity into the way of peace.

The Light that would go on to remain with His people forever.

LECTIO DIVINA

Take a moment to breathe deeply. Close your eyes and invite Holy Spirit to speak to you as you read God's Word. Your invitation can be as simple as, "God, I recognize that in this moment, as in all moments, I am in your presence. Speak for your servant is listening."

READ:

And you, my child, will be called a prophet of the Most High; for you will go on before the Lord to prepare the way for him, 77 to give his people the knowledge of salvation through the forgiveness of their sins, 78 because of the tender mercy of our God, by which the rising sun will come to us from heaven 79 to shine on those living in darkness and in the shadow of death, to guide our feet into the path of peace. Luke 1:76-79 [NIV]

Take a moment to allow the Scripture to sink in. Now, go back and read it two more times. Each time, read slowly and pay special attention to any word or phrase that sticks out to you.

Ask Holy Spirit to reveal to you why (if any) word or phrase stuck out during your reading. Use the space below to journal your thoughts.

WEEK 1: DAY FIVE

But you, Bethlehem Ephrathah, though you are small among the clans of Judah, out of you will come for me one who will be ruler over Israel, whose origins are from of old, from ancient times. Micah 5:2-5 [NIV]

***

One of my favorite elements of the Christmas story is its cast of characters. In most other stories, the main characters of Christmas would be supporting roles. A young virgin girl. A middle-class carpenter. Blue-collar shepherds. A small town the rest of the country had all but forgotten.

God chooses this group to reveal His redemptive plan to the world. Conventional wisdom would say that statesmen, academics, and the affluent are who you should pull close if you want to make an impact. However, in the Kingdom of God, the posture of your heart, not your acumen or your position in society, determines the ultimate impact your life will make.

1 Corinthian 1:27 says, "But God chose the foolish things of the world to shame the wise; God chose the weak things of the world to shame the strong." [NIV]

When you feel inadequate, insecure, and unimportant in life, remember 1 Corinthians 1:27. For the value of your life is not determined by the power you wield, nor the adoration you inspire; the value of your life is found in the love God has for you.

When you feel strong, mighty, and essential, remember 1 Corinthians 1:27. Be reminded that God is not looking to you to accomplish His plans as if you have the special skills or power He needs to bring about His will. God calls upon you to be gentle and humble in heart (Matthew 11:29) so that you can actively participate in His redemptive work in the world.

God doesn't need you to participate.

God wants you to participate.

What He calls you to do may feel out of reach or foolish for your current stage of life. It may affect your status in society and put you at risk of ridicule from others. Just like it did for Mary and Joseph. Do not allow this to stop you from the work God has called you toward.

It is better to be foolish for God than a fool dressed like a wise man.

For, in the end, all will be revealed.

LECTIO DIVINA

Take a moment to breathe deeply. Close your eyes and invite Holy Spirit to speak to you as you read God's Word. Your invitation can be as simple as, "God, I recognize that in this moment, as in all moments, I am in your presence. Speak for your servant is listening."

READ:

But you, Bethlehem Ephrathah, though you are small among the clans of Judah, out of you will come for me one who will be ruler over Israel, whose origins are from of old, from ancient times. Micah 5:2-5 [NIV]

Take a moment to allow the Scripture to sink in. Now, go back and read it two more times. Each time, read slowly and pay special attention to any word or phrase that sticks out to you.

Ask Holy Spirit to reveal to you why (if any) word or phrase stuck out during your reading. Use the space below to journal your thoughts.

_____

_____

_____

_____

_____

_____

_____

WEEK 1: DAY SIX

For the perishable must clothe itself with the imperishable, and the mortal with immortality. 54 When the perishable has been clothed with the imperishable, and the mortal with immortality, then the saying that is written will come true: "Death has been swallowed up in victory." 55 "Where, O death, is your victory? Where, O death, is your sting?" 56 The sting of death is sin, and the power of sin is the law. **57 But thanks be to God! He gives us the victory through our Lord Jesus Christ. 58 Therefore, my dear brothers and sisters, stand firm. Let nothing move you. Always give yourselves fully to the work of the Lord, because you know that your   labor   in   the   Lord   is   not   in   vain.** 1 Corinthians 15:53-58 [NIV]

***

Viktor Frankl was an Austrian psychiatrist and a survivor of four Nazi concentration camps, at which he lost his father, mother, brother, and wife over the course of three years.

Man's Search For Meaning is the autobiographical account of Frankl's experiences in the camps. One of the observations he makes in the book is related to the increase in deaths that occurred in one of the camps between Christmas 1944 and New Year 1945.

Frankl theorized that the increased death rate came not as a result of more demanding working conditions or a lessening of rations, as one might expect, but because of the naïve hope that the prisoners had of being freed by Christmas. According to

Frankl, a person's inner strength in the camp was directly tied to their ability to find purpose and meaning in life outside of the camp itself.

If a prisoner's hope relied solely on the future goal of freedom or on relief from the inhumane state of affairs, then this hope was not only untenable, it could not provide one with the resolve needed to persevere.

"He who has a why to live for can bear with almost any how," says Frankl, quoting Nietzsche.

For the Christian, our great hope comes not as a key that unlocks the chains of suffering but as a suffering servant who opens the door to everlasting life with the Creator.

The world's wisdom says to place our hope in political power, riches, or influence. Many people have followed this path throughout history, and their hope was eventually replaced with disappointment, discouragement, and desperation.

The birth of Christ reminds us that God's methods often differ from our own. He does not need to follow the paths laid out by the world's wisdom. The Kingdom of God has come and will continue to come because of the Babe in the Manger.

This gives the Christian a "why" to live for that is greater than anything the world has to offer. Our "why" encompasses and extends beyond the confines of this present age. Our "why" is the reconciliation and redemption of creation itself (Rom 8:18-20). We have confidence knowing that in the Lord, our labor is not in vain (1 Cor 15:58). This confidence enables us to persevere when the work God has called us to is hopeless by the measuring stick the world uses.

We abound in hope (Rom 15:13) because our "why" is the reign and rule of Jesus Christ, wherein God dwells with His people and wipes away every tear from their eye (Rev 21:3-4).

LECTIO DIVINA

Take a moment to breathe deeply. Close your eyes and invite Holy Spirit to speak to you as you read God's Word. Your invitation can be as simple as, "God, I recognize that in this moment, as in all moments, I am in your presence. Speak for your servant is listening."

READ:
And I heard a loud voice from the throne saying, "Look! God's dwelling place is now among the people, and he will dwell with them. They will be his people, and God himself will be with them and be their God. 4 'He will wipe every tear from their eyes. There will be no more death' or mourning or crying or pain, for the old order of things has passed away." Rev 21:3-4 [NIV]

Take a moment to allow the Scripture to sink in. Now, go back and read it two more times. Each time, read slowly and pay special attention to any word or phrase that sticks out to you.

Ask Holy Spirit to reveal to you why (if any) word or phrase stuck out during your reading. Use the space below to journal your thoughts.

_____

_____

_____

_____

_____

_____

_____

WEEK 1: DAY SEVEN

Worship the LORD in the splendor of his holiness; tremble before him, all the earth. 10 Say among the nations, "The LORD reigns." The world is firmly established, it cannot be moved; he will judge the peoples with equity. 11 Let the heavens rejoice, let the earth be glad; let the sea resound, and all that is in it. 12 Let the fields be jubilant, and everything in them; let all the trees of the forest sing for joy. **13 Let all creation rejoice before the LORD, for he comes, he comes to judge the earth. He will judge the world in righteousness and the peoples in his faithfulness.** Psalm 96:9-13 [NIV]

***

Christmas is a season filled with anticipation for most people. I suspect this feeling germinates for most of us in childhood. As kids, we were filled with anticipation as we eagerly looked forward to Christmas morning. We couldn't wait to jump out of bed, rush over to the Christmas tree, and tear through the wrapping paper in a flurry of excitement.

This anticipation was always hope-filled. We sized up each box, anticipating the goodness of what was inside. I don't remember ever picking up a box as a child, fearing whether the contents inside would harm me. Instead, I remember being packed to the brim with curiosity, wondering what my parents had prepared for me.

As an adult, the anticipation of Christmas tends to look different. Perhaps we still anticipate some gifts. We may anticipate what interactions with family and friends will be like, the good and the bad. We likely anticipate the break from the monotony of our work and toil. For some, we also anticipate the pain and heartache of sitting at the table, knowing that one of the seats will be empty this year.

The reality of anticipation is that it can be filled with joy and wonder, and it can be filled with fear and regret. For many, anticipation falls into the latter category this time of year.

As followers of Christ, there is an anticipation we must not forget, no matter how we feel about the modern, western celebrations that bear the name of our Savior. We are to anticipate the return of Jesus.

The early church faced much persecution, the likes of which most of us cannot fathom. Rather than let this persecution fill them with fearful anticipation, they chose to anticipate the return of Christ. A common greeting amongst the church was Maranatha (1 Cor 16:22) which meant, "Come, Lord Jesus!"

This greeting was a way of reminding each other that, no matter what was happening in the here and now, there was a day of redemption coming. Just as Christ came, He will come again. Only this time, He's not coming as a helpless babe but as a righteous ruler to judge all the earth with equity.

Jesus is coming to restore what's been tarnished. He's coming to give life where the pain of death has been felt. He's coming to heal disease, free the captives, and give sight to the blind.

Jesus is coming to reign and rule. Like when we were kids, the Advent season should build anticipation in us, knowing that in just a few short moments, we will unwrap the temporary and see in all of its glory eternity in the Kingdom of God.

Maranatha!

LECTIO DIVINA

Take a moment to breathe deeply. Close your eyes and invite Holy Spirit to speak to you as you read God's Word. Your invitation can be as simple as, "God, I recognize that in this moment, as in all moments, I am in your presence. Speak for your servant is listening."

READ:

Worship the LORD in the splendor of his holiness; tremble before him, all the earth. 10 Say among the nations, "The LORD reigns." The world is firmly established, it cannot be moved; he will judge the peoples with equity. 11 Let the heavens rejoice, let the earth be glad; let the sea resound, and all that is in it. 12 Let the fields be jubilant, and everything in them; let all the trees of the forest sing for joy. **13 Let all creation rejoice before the LORD, for he comes, he comes to judge the earth. He will judge the world in righteousness and the peoples in his faithfulness"**. Psalm 96:9-13 [NIV]

Take a moment to allow the Scripture to sink in. Now, go back and read it two more times. Each time, read slowly and pay special attention to any word or phrase that sticks out to you.

Ask Holy Spirit to reveal to you why (if any) word or phrase stuck out during your reading. Use the space below to journal your thoughts.

_____

_____

_____

_____

_____

_____

PEACE

Keep your eyes on the prince of peace, the one who doesn't cling to his divine power; the one who refuses to turn stones into bread, jump from great heights and rule with great power; the one who says, "Blessed are the poor, the gentle, those who mourn, and those who hunger and thirst for righteousness; blessed are the merciful, the pure in heart, the peacemakers and those who are persecuted in the cause of uprightness" (see Matt. 5:3-11); the one who touches the lame, the crippled, and the blind; the one who speaks words of forgiveness and encouragement; the one who dies alone, rejected and despised. Keep your eyes on him who becomes poor with the poor, weak with the weak, and who is rejected with the rejected. He is the source of all peace.[1]

-Henri Nouwen

---

[1] *Nouwen, H., & Durback, R. (1997, December 29). Seeds of Hope: A Henri Nouwen Reader (1rst EDITION BY BANTAM BOOKS). Image Books.*

WEEK 2: DAY ONE

Suddenly a great company of the heavenly host appeared with the angel, praising God and saying, 14 "Glory to God in the highest heaven, and on earth peace (shalowm) to those on whom his favor rests." Luke 2:13-14 [NIV]

***

The modern western definition of peace differs significantly from the Hebrew definition of peace. We tend to think of peace as one nation's ideologies and values being the standard others are forced to live under. It's a lack of strife between opposing parties—the time between wars.

Peace in the west has its roots in the Greco-Roman definition of peace. The English language gets the word peace from the Latin word pax. For the Roman people, pax was the cessation of hostility between groups. Often this pax came because one of the groups was conquered by the other, i.e., the Pax Romana.

The Hebrew definition of peace, called shalowm, is quite different. Rabbi Robert I. Kahn of Houston, Texas, explains the distinctions between the Roman idea of peace (pax) and Hebrew shalowm in this way:

"One can dictate a peace; shalom is a mutual agreement. Peace is a temporary pact; shalom is a permanent agreement. Peace can be negative, the absence of commotion. Shalom is positive, the presence of serenity. Peace can be partial; shalom is whole."

Shalowm is a wholeness of being. A perfect harmony with all things. It is the original order intended by the Creator.

The first picture of shalowm in the Bible is found in the first few chapters. The Garden of Eden was a place of shalowm, not because conflict was absent, but because Adam and Eve walked in right relationship with God. This right relationship enabled them to operate in harmony with the created order by cultivating the land.

True Biblical peace isn't subtractive, as in it doesn't remove conflict. Instead, it gives wholeness in the midst of it. The creation narrative reveals a harmony, a shalowm, that is present in places of conflict.

Shalowm says opposing forces can operate in harmony with one another. Light and darkness both have their place in creation. One does not obliterate the other; God sets boundaries to establish how they will operate in harmony with one another. The dry land has its boundary, as does the sea, and because of those boundaries shalowm is present, and life springs forth from both.

Modern peace (pax) is the absence of conflict. Shalowm peace is the presence of God that produces harmony amid conflict.

This is the type of peace promised to those who follow Christ. Jesus is our peace (Ephesians 2:14), not because He has removed conflict from our lives but because He has provided us the path to maintain wholeness amid the devastation.

Do not be deceived; true peace will not come on the back of an elected official, from a miracle drug, or technological advancements.

True peace comes from the Babe in the manger.

LECTIO DIVINA

Take a moment to breathe deeply. Close your eyes and invite Holy Spirit to speak to you as you read God's Word. Your invitation can be as simple as, "God, I recognize that in this moment, as in all moments, I am in your presence. Speak for your servant is listening."

READ:

Suddenly a great company of the heavenly host appeared with the angel, praising God and saying, 14 "Glory to God in the highest heaven, and on earth peace (shalowm) to those on whom his favor rests." Luke 2:13-14 [NIV]

Take a moment to allow the Scripture to sink in. Now, go back and read it two more times. Each time, read slowly and pay special attention to any word or phrase that sticks out to you.

Ask Holy Spirit to reveal to you why (if any) word or phrase stuck out during your reading. Use the space below to journal your thoughts.

_____

_____

_____

_____

_____

_____

_____

WEEK 2: DAY TWO

The wolf will live with the lamb, the leopard will lie down with the goat, the calf and the lion and the yearling together; and a little child will lead them. 7 The cow will feed with the bear, their young will lie down together, and the lion will eat straw like the ox. 8 The infant will play near the cobra's den, and the young child will put its hand into the viper's nest. 9 They will neither harm nor destroy on all my holy mountain, for the earth will be filled with the knowledge of the LORD as the waters cover the sea. Isaiah 11:6-9 [NIV]

***

The first twelve chapters of the book of Isaiah paint a picture of what the Kingdom of God will be like under the reign of the Messianic King. One of the more startling revelations comes in chapter eleven. According to Isaiah, the Messiah's power won't stop at the removal of evil and the reign of justice; his power will cause the wolf to live with the lamb and the leopard to lie next to the goat.

This is a startling revelation because, of course, wolves do not co-exist with lambs. They kill them. Leopards do not lie down next to goats. They eat them. If you've ever observed the animal kingdom's relationship between predators and prey, you know it is a violent, deadly relationship. The predator consumes the prey to stay alive. According to Isaiah, this reality will no longer exist in the coming Kingdom of God.

When Christ returns to fulfill His work, not only will there be peace between predator and prey, but the peace will be such that even a child will be able to lead them, which acts as a nod to the power and authority God gave Adam and Eve in the Garden of Eden.

This will be possible because the very nature of the animals will be changed. Verse 7 says the lion will eat straw like the ox. In its current fallen state, the lion must consume the flesh of its prey to survive, but in the Kingdom of God, its very nature will be brought back into harmony with God's original created order.

One does not have to use their imagination much to see how the animal kingdom's predator and prey dynamics exist in human society. Caste systems, the abuse of political power, racism, sexism, violence, and the like all reveal the desperate state in which much of the human population has lived since the dawn of time.

This is not to say that abuses of power and violence are excused because of the fallen state of humanity. Scripture is clear that any offense done to a person is an offense to the imago dei inside of them and, thereby, an offense against God, Himself.

It's worth noting that the Messiah's reign and rule does not negate the differences between predator and prey. The wolf does not become a lamb, nor does the lamb become a wolf. They maintain the distinctions that define them. Only these differences will no longer breed strife and violence between them; rather, they will complement each other, bringing a wholeness (shalowm) to creation itself.

The Kingdom of God will be filled with variety and difference. It will not be homogenous. There will be different shades of color, types of people, and groups that were once enemies of each other.

All things will resemble a beautiful tapestry, the different strands woven together in peace with one thread tying them all together: the knowledge of God.

LECTIO DIVINA

Take a moment to breathe deeply. Close your eyes and invite Holy Spirit to speak to you as you read God's Word. Your invitation can be as simple as, "God, I recognize that in this moment, as in all moments, I am in your presence. Speak for your servant is listening."

READ:
The wolf will live with the lamb, the leopard will lie down with the goat, the calf and the lion and the yearling together; and a little child will lead them. 7 The cow will feed with the bear, their young will lie down together, and the lion will eat straw like the ox. 8 The infant will play near the cobra's den, and the young child will put its hand into the viper's nest. 9 They will neither harm nor destroy on all my holy mountain, for the earth will be filled with the knowledge of the LORD as the waters cover the sea. Isaiah 11:6-9 [NIV]

Take a moment to allow the Scripture to sink in. Now, go back and read it two more times. Each time, read slowly and pay special attention to any word or phrase that sticks out to you.

Ask Holy Spirit to reveal to you why (if any) word or phrase stuck out during your reading. Use the space below to journal your thoughts.

WEEK 2: DAY THREE

Therefore my people will know my name; therefore in that day they will know that it is I who foretold it. Yes, it is I." 7 How beautiful on the mountains are the feet of those who bring good news, who proclaim peace, who bring good tidings, who proclaim salvation, who say to Zion, "Your God reigns!" Isaiah 52:6-8 [NIV]

***

Isaiah 52 is a prophecy that arrives while the Jewish people are under oppression from Babylon. Many of God's people had been taken away from their homeland and forced into exile. And for those living in captivity, the sovereign authority of the world seemed to be Babylon, not God.

The story of the Babylonian Exile parallels another time of great oppression in Israel's history: when they were slaves in Egypt. On the surface, the Pharaoh seemed to be the ruler of the world, just like the King of Babylon. Egypt appeared to hold limitless power, just like Babylon.

However, there is one key difference between the Babylonian Exile and Israel's slavery in Egypt: the Babylonian Exile came as a result of Israel's sin (2 Chronicles 36:14-21), whereas Israel's slavery in Egypt came as a result of Egypt's sin (Exodus 9:27).

This is significant because it reveals the two ways sin brings devastation. Sometimes, it is the sinner who suffers its penalty.

Other times, those who are sinned against are forced to pay its price.

In the case of Israel's history, sin had twice separated the people from God's presence and subjected them to foreign oppression. And, in both cases, it was the power of God alone that could free them.

The Exodus became the hallmark of God's power and care for the Israelites, exhibited His authority in the world, and revealed how He would come to dwell with His people. And now, amidst Babylonian oppression, Isaiah declared once again, **"Your God reigns!"**

This is the same imagery the early Christians used to explain what Jesus's death had won for the people of God. They claimed that the forgiveness of sins through the work of Christ had overthrown the world's enslaving powers and brought the people of God peace.

It did not matter whether or not the sin had occurred at the hands of the oppressed or from the oppressor; sin, and thereby death, would no longer have power over those who chose to live under God's rule.

When Jesus prays, "Your kingdom come." this is precisely what He beckons. He is calling for the day when those who sin, and those who are sinned against, are no longer subjected to the penalty of sin. He's calling for the day when those separated from God will be permitted to return to God's presence where there is perfect peace.

This perfect peace will not exist in some ethereal place disconnected from reality.

This peace will exist on earth as it is in heaven.

41

LECTIO DIVINA

Take a moment to breathe deeply. Close your eyes and invite Holy Spirit to speak to you as you read God's Word. Your invitation can be as simple as, "God, I recognize that in this moment, as in all moments, I am in your presence. Speak for your servant is listening."

READ:

Therefore my people will know my name; therefore in that day they will know that it is I who foretold it. Yes, it is I." 7 How beautiful on the mountains are the feet of those who bring good news, who proclaim peace, who bring good tidings, who proclaim salvation, who say to Zion, "Your God reigns!" Isaiah 52:6-8 [NIV]

Take a moment to allow the Scripture to sink in. Now, go back and read it two more times. Each time, read slowly and pay special attention to any word or phrase that sticks out to you.

Ask Holy Spirit to reveal to you why (if any) word or phrase stuck out during your reading. Use the space below to journal your thoughts.

_____

_____

_____

_____

_____

_____

_____

_____

WEEK 2: DAY FOUR

Hear us, Shepherd of Israel, you who lead Joseph like a flock. You who sit enthroned between the cherubim, shine forth 2 before Ephraim, Benjamin and Manasseh. Awaken your might; come and save us. 3 Restore us, O God; make your face shine on us, that we may be saved. 4 How long, LORD God Almighty, will your anger smolder against the prayers of your people? 5 You have fed them with the bread of tears; you have made them drink tears by the bowlful. 6 You have made us an object of derision to our neighbors, and our enemies mock us. 7 Restore us, God Almighty; make your face shine on us, that we may be saved. Psalm 80:1-7 [NIV]

***

It's easy to breeze past Scriptures like Psalm 80. We may assume there is little to glean from them since our current situation differs significantly from the captivity they were experiencing.

Imagine what it would be like to live in a land full of desperation and despair. Turmoil and pain seem to be the currency by which the culture thrives. Hate, vitriol, and violence are used as weapons to turn people groups against each other.

All one needs to do is live through one election cycle in the west to see that not much has changed thousands of years later. Like ancient Israel, we, too, cry out desperately for a savior.

Desperation can be incredibly dangerous when it positions flawed human beings as the solution to the world's problems.

And yet, desperation can also be the current that pulls us into a deeper, richer long for the soon-coming King.

The longings we all have for something better, our desires for injustice to be corrected, for pain to cease, and for unending life come from the goodness God has placed inside us (Eccl 3:11).

They are longings for true peace.

When I read Psalm 80, I feel my soul's desperation rise. I become aware of my desperate need for a Savior. One who can deliver me from the pain and heartache that my own hands, and the hands of others, bring into my life.

I long for the Messiah who supersedes political parties, national lines, and socioeconomic class systems.

I am desperate for the return of the Christ who saves.

LECTIO DIVINA

Take a moment to breathe deeply. Close your eyes and invite Holy Spirit to speak to you as you read God's Word. Your invitation can as be simple as, "God, I recognize that in this moment, as in all moments, I am in your presence. Speak for your servant is listening."

READ:
Hear us, Shepherd of Israel, you who lead Joseph like a flock. You who sit enthroned between the cherubim, shine forth 2 before Ephraim, Benjamin and Manasseh. Awaken your might; come and save us. 3 Restore us, O God; make your face shine on us, that we may be saved. 4 How long, LORD God Almighty, will your anger smolder against the prayers of your people? 5 You have fed them with the bread of tears; you have made them drink tears by the bowlful. 6 You have made us an object of derision to our neighbors, and our enemies mock us. 7 Restore us, God Almighty; make your face shine on us, that we may be saved. Psalm 80:1-7 [NIV]

Take a moment to allow the Scripture to sink in. Now, go back and read it two more times. Each time, read slowly and pay special attention to any word or phrase that sticks out to you.

Ask Holy Spirit to reveal to you why (if any) word or phrase stuck out during your reading. Use the space below to journal your thoughts.

_____

_____

_____

_____

_____

_____

WEEK 2: DAY FIVE

Peace I leave with you; my peace I give you. I do not give to you as the world gives. Do not let your hearts be troubled and do not be afraid. John 14:27 [NIV]

***

Modern definitions of peace are often tied to a thing. We assume that if we just had enough money in our bank account, or if we just had the right type of life partner, or if we just had a better career, or a family, or fame, then, finally, we would have peace.

The great deception of our day is that peace is contingent on what you can attain rather than on receiving what's been given to you.

As long as your peace (shalowm) depends on your money, your sexuality, your social status, or anything else you look to other than Christ, your peace will be fractured.

It will be a light and momentary peace.

The time between conflicts that happen in life.

It will be a pseudo-peace.

This is because shalowm does not come from something; it comes from someone: Christ. It is in Jesus that we have been given peace from God (Phil 4:7) and peace with God (Romans 5:1).

This peace does not leave us when trials and tribulations come. Rather it enables us to stand on a solid foundation (Matthew 7:24-29) when the storms of life bear down on us and those we love.

Any other foundation we try to build our peace on will ultimately fail us because it lacks the power to grant peace. As the old hymn goes, all other ground is sinking sand.

It is Christ alone who can give peace.

Jesus says in John 16:33 [NIV], "I have told you these things, so that in me you may have peace. In this world you will have trouble. But take heart! I have overcome the world.""

Even when we experience significant troubles in the world, which Jesus makes clear we'll experience, Christians can take heart because shalowm, wholeness, and harmony, reside in us and with us because of Jesus.

This is because true peace is not contingent on a lack of conflict; it rests on the shoulders of a person.

"But now in Christ Jesus you who once were far away have been brought near by the blood of Christ. For he himself is our peace," Ephesians 2:13-14a [NIV]

You will have no peace until you know the One who is peace.

LECTIO DIVINA

Take a moment to breathe deeply. Close your eyes and invite Holy Spirit to speak to you as you read God's Word. Your invitation can be as simple as, "God, I recognize that in this moment, as in all moments, I am in your presence. Speak for your servant is listening."

READ:
Peace I leave with you; my peace I give you. I do not give to you as the world gives. Do not let your hearts be troubled and do not be afraid. John 14:27 [NIV]

"But now in Christ Jesus you who once were far away have been brought near by the blood of Christ. For he himself is our peace," Ephesians 2:13-14a [NIV]

Take a moment to allow the Scriptures to sink in. Now, go back and read them two more times. Each time, read slowly, and pay special attention to any word or phrase that sticks out to you.

Ask Holy Spirit to reveal to you why (if any) word or phrase stuck out during your reading. Use the space below to journal your thoughts.

_____

_____

_____

_____

_____

WEEK 2: DAY SIX

Do not be anxious about anything, but in every situation, by prayer and petition, with thanksgiving, present your requests to God. 7 And the peace of God, which transcends all understanding, will guard your hearts and your minds in Christ Jesus. Philippians 4:6-7 [NIV]

***

When I was a child, my mother prayed Philippians 4:6 over me on a near-nightly basis. I suffered from anxiety about what the future may hold as a kid, though I didn't have that word at the time.

For years, almost every night before bed, I would get a sinking feeling in the pit of my stomach that something terrible would happen. It caused me to feel restless and unable to sleep. I would toss and turn and, eventually, would be overcome with tears.

Every time my mom would walk into my room. She would sit on the edge of my bed. Then, she would pray over me, and at some point in the prayer, she would faithfully say, "Lord, I ask that your peace which surpasses all understanding, would guard Paul's heart and mind in Jesus."

It wasn't until I got older, and started reading the Bible, that I realized my mom was praying Philippians 4 over me. Her prayer, and this Scripture, have proven to be a mainstay in my life and ministry over the last thirty years.

It would seem I'm far from the only one who has an affinity for the Apostle Paul's words found in Philippians 4. In 2014, Amazon released data that revealed that Philippians 4:6-7 was the most highlighted passage on Kindle in the Bible.[1]

We all crave peace, particularly when we feel things aren't going our way or when circumstances leave us confused and brokenhearted. The power of the promise found in Philippians 4 is that we can have God's peace that surpasses our understanding.

Even when life doesn't make sense, when there seems to be no greater purpose for the events that happened, when there is no logical reason for us to have peace, the peace of God can and will guard our hearts and minds in Christ Jesus.

Of course, you only get the promise of verse 7 by living verse 6. Before the Apostle Paul says we can have the peace of God, he instructs us to pray and make our requests known to God in every situation with a posture of thanksgiving.

This way of praying may sound intimidating, but it doesn't have to be. As Father John Chapman said, "Pray as you can, not as you can't."

God does not have a time chart waiting for you to clock in.

This type of prayer life is a simple invitation that you extend to God to be a part of your life through the posture of your heart.

It is walking through your day, aware of God's presence, and seeking His will for whatever circumstance you encounter.

Sometimes, that will mean speaking aloud as if God were standing next to you. Other times, it will be searching your heart to discern what God is saying. That's it.

That's the simple path to the peace of God that surpasses understanding.

---

[1] Meyer, R. (2014, November 3). *The Most Popular Passages in Books, According to Kindle Data.* The Atlantic. Retrieved October 3, 2022, from https://www.theatlantic.com/technology/archive/2014/11/the-passages-that-readers-love/381373/

LECTIO DIVINA

Take a moment to breathe deeply. Close your eyes and invite Holy Spirit to speak to you as you read God's Word. Your invitation can be as simple as, "God, I recognize that in this moment, as in all moments, I am in your presence. Speak for your servant is listening."

READ:

Do not be anxious about anything, but in every situation, by prayer and petition, with thanksgiving, present your requests to God. 7 And the peace of God, which transcends all understanding, will guard your hearts and your minds in Christ Jesus. Philippians 4:6-7 [NIV]

Take a moment to allow the Scripture to sink in. Now, go back and read it two more times. Each time, read slowly and pay special attention to any word or phrase that sticks out to you.

Ask Holy Spirit to reveal to you why (if any) word or phrase stuck out during your reading. Use the space below to journal your thoughts.

_____

_____

_____

_____

_____

_____

_____

_____

WEEK 2: DAY SEVEN

This is what the LORD says: "When seventy years are completed for Babylon, I will come to you and fulfill my good promise to bring you back to this place. 11 For I know the plans I have for you," declares the LORD, "plans to prosper you and not to harm you, plans to give you hope and a future. 12 Then you will call on me and come and pray to me, and I will listen to you. 13 You will seek me and find me when you seek me with all your heart. Jeremiah 29:10-13 [NIV]

***

Imagine, out of nowhere, the entire landscape and culture of your nation changing overnight. This is what happened to Israel. Some Jews found themselves living in a foreign land. Others found that friends and family were no longer within reach. They were a disconnected, disjointed, deeply wounded people.

And it is at this time that God sends the message of hope found in Jeremiah 29. If you grew up in the American church in the 1990s like I did, you probably heard some boneheaded preacher use that Scripture to justify the cancer of consumerism in the church.

They likely said that God wants the people of God to prosper, and then they defined prosperity as riches, comforts, and influence. This is a gross misapplication of this Scripture.

The frustration I have toward them isn't that they oversold the promise of Jeremiah 29, but that they undersold its power.

The word that most English editions of the Bible translate as prosperity in Jeremiah 29:11 is actually the Hebrew word shalowm. God promises His people that His plan for them is harmony and completeness.

God doesn't promise to make them rich, He promises to make them whole.

This promise first and foremost was made to the people of God in captivity in Babylon, but I think it also reveals how God interacts with His children. After all, 2 Corinthians 1:20 says the promises of God find their yes in Jesus.

What this verse says to me is that even when I find myself in an unexpected place in life, I can stand on a solid foundation and declare that shalowm is possible in my upside-down world.

How does this happen? Through prayer and through active participation in God's redemptive work in the world.

In Jeremiah 29:7, right before the promise found in verse 11, God instructs Israel to "...seek the [shalowm] of the city to which I have carried you into exile. Pray to the LORD for it, because if it [shalowm], you too will [shalowm]."

Don't miss the potency of what God tells Israel to do. God says that the way for them to find peace in their lifetime was to seek peace for the people who ransacked their country, killed their countrymen, and took them as slaves to a foreign land.

I believe this is why Jesus says in Matthew 5:9, "Blessed are the peacemakers, for they will be called children of God." [NIV]

During the Advent season, we must remember that it was when we were still enemies of God (Romans 5:10) that He sent His Son to us so that we may be reconciled back to Him.

We must remember that the Christ child came to bring us peace and that we are now called to bring peace to the world.

53

LECTIO DIVINA

Take a moment to breathe deeply. Close your eyes and invite Holy Spirit to speak to you as you read God's Word. Your invitation can be as simple as, "God, I recognize that in this moment, as in all moments, I am in your presence. Speak for your servant is listening."

READ:

"For I know the plans I have for you," declares the LORD, "plans to prosper you and not to harm you, plans to give you hope and a future. 12 Then you will call on me and come and pray to me, and   I   will   listen   to   you." Jeremiah 29:11-12 [NIV]

"Also, seek the peace and prosperity of the city to which I have carried you into exile. Pray to the LORD for it, because if it prospers, you too will prosper." Jeremiah 29:7 [NIV]

Take a moment to allow the Scriptures to sink in. Now, go back and read each two more times. Each time, read slowly and pay special attention to any word or phrase that sticks out to you.

Ask Holy Spirit to reveal to you why (if any) word or phrase stuck out during your reading. Use the space below to journal your thoughts.

_____

_____

_____

_____

_____

J O Y

"Donatus, this is a cheerful world indeed as I see it from my fair garden, under the shadow of my vines. But if I could ascend some high mountain, and look out over the wide lands, you know very well that I should see: brigands on the highways, pirates on the seas, armies fighting, cities burning, in the amphitheaters men murdered to please applauding crowds, selfishness and cruelty and misery and despair under all roofs. It is a bad world, Donatus, an incredibly bad world.

"But I have discovered in the midst of it a company of quiet and holy people who have learned a great secret. They have found a joy which is a thousand times better than any of the pleasures of our sinful life. They are despised and persecuted, but they care not: they are masters of their souls. They have overcome the world. These people, Donatus, are the Christians, —
and I am one of them."[1]

-Cyprian of Carthage

---

[1] in a letter to his friend Donatus, 249 AD.

WEEK 3: DAY ONE

I delight greatly in the LORD; my soul rejoices in my God. For he has clothed me with garments of salvation and arrayed me in a robe of his righteousness, as a bridegroom adorns his head like a priest, and as a bride adorns herself with her jewels. 11 For as the soil makes the sprout come up and a garden causes seeds to grow, so the Sovereign LORD will make righteousness and praise spring up before all nations. Isaiah 61:10-11 [NIV]

***

Some 700 years before the birth of Jesus, the prophet Isaiah wrote about the Messiah who was to come. He described him as one whom the LORD had "anointed to bring good news to the poor...to bandage the brokenhearted...to proclaim liberty to the prisoners...and freedom to the captives." [1]

In short, Messiah would bring joy to the world.

Modern depictions of joy during the Christmas season would have us believe that joy comes from festive food, drink, and presents under the tree. Joy in our day seems to result from festive activities like gazing at Christmas lights or honoring traditions with friends and family.

While none of these are bad things, they are wholly incapable

---

[1] Isaiah 61:1 (author's paraphrase of modern translations)

of producing the type of joy available to Christians (1 Peter 1:8-9). They may produce temporary happiness, but that happiness is only the outer crust of the deep, rich joy available to those who submit to Christ.

Joy is a feeling deep in your soul produced by the Holy Spirit (Galatians 5:22-23) and anchored by faith in Jesus's victory that brought salvation to all who believe (1 Peter 1:8-9).

The critical differences between happiness and joy are that happiness is a temporary feeling brought on by activities one delights in. In contrast, joy is a permanent state held by one's belief in the steadfast power and victory of Christ Jesus.

This state can and does produce good feelings, much like happiness, but those feelings arise not out of an activity the person does but out of the work of Christ.

This is why happiness fades after the novelty of the activity wears off, while joy remains steadfast because the work of Christ is eternal. It's how the Apostle Paul can command us to "Rejoice in the LORD always, rejoice!" (Philippians 4:4), and it not be a fool's errand.

We really can be joyful in all things.

One cannot live in a blissful state of happiness in this life, but unceasing joy is made available to all who call on the name of Jesus. This joy comes as a result of keeping one's eyes fixated on the salvation that Christ won for us.

Traditions will falter.

Festivities will lose their appeal.

But the joy of the LORD can forever be your strength.

LECTIO DIVINA

Take a moment to breathe deeply. Close your eyes and invite Holy Spirit to speak to you as you read God's Word. Your invitation can be as simple as, "God, I recognize that in this moment, as in all moments, I am in your presence. Speak for your servant is listening."

READ:

I delight greatly in the LORD; my soul rejoices in my God. For he has clothed me with garments of salvation and arrayed me in a robe of his righteousness, as a bridegroom adorns his head like a priest, and as a bride adorns herself with her jewels. 11 For as the soil makes the sprout come up and a garden causes seeds to grow, so the Sovereign LORD will make righteousness and praise spring up before all nations. Isaiah 61:10-11 [NIV]

Take a moment to allow the Scripture to sink in. Now, go back and read it two more times. Each time, read slowly and pay special attention to any word or phrase that sticks out to you.

Ask Holy Spirit to reveal to you why (if any) word or phrase stuck out during your reading. Use the space below to journal your thoughts.

_____

_____

_____

_____

_____

_____

WEEK 3: DAY TWO

But the angel said to them, "Do not be afraid. I bring you good news that will cause great joy for all the people. 11 Today in the town of David a Savior has been born to you; he is the Messiah, the Lord. Luke 2:10-11 [NIV]

***

In a letter in 1944, J.R.R Tolkien, Lord of the Rings author, coined the term "eucatastrophe." [1] The word combines the Greek prefix eu, meaning good, and catastrophe, which refers to a plot's unraveling or dramatic conclusion.

A eucatastrophe is a grace that enters into a story unexpectedly, the turn for the better no one saw coming when all hope of victory seemed lost.

If you have read Lord of the Rings, then you know this to be moments like Gandalf returning from death as Gandalf The White, or if you are familiar with modern cinema, it's the Avengers rising to defeat Thanos in Avengers: Endgame. I also think Lebron's block in 2016 and the resulting Cleveland Cavaliers Championship was a eucatastrophe. [2]

---

[1] Tolkien, J. R. R. (1981, October 3). *The Letters of J.R.R. Tolkien*. Allen & Unwin. "Letter 88"
[2] The Warriors blew a 3-1 lead. (https://www.youtube.com/watch?v=-zd62MxKXp8)

The concept of eucatastrophe is so powerful and used so frequently in modern storytelling that many deem it cliché and entirely unrealistic. Tolkien believed that a eucatastrophe holds power, not because it's unrealistic, but because it identifies the mechanism by which God redeemed humanity.

"I coined the word 'eucatastrophe': the sudden happy turn in a story which pierces you with a joy that brings tears... And I was there led to the view that it produces its peculiar effect because it is a sudden glimpse of Truth, your whole nature chained in material cause and effect, the chain of death, feels a sudden relief as if a major limb out of joint had suddenly snapped back. It perceives – if the story has literary 'truth' on the second plane (....) – that this is indeed how things really do work in the Great World for which our nature is made." [1]

According to Tolkien, Jesus's birth marks the first eucatastrophe in human history. The advent of Christ is the entrance of unmerited grace into mankind's story, a story whose ending seemed to be final defeat; yet suddenly gives way to a whisper of hope. This whisper of hope then grows into a full declaration of victory through the work of Christ.

"The birth of Christ is the Eucatastrophe of Man's history. The Resurrection is the Eucatastrophe of the story of the Incarnation. This story begins and ends in joy." [2]

This is why the angels declare that joy has come to all people.

The birth of Jesus is the crack in the clouds that pierces the darkness of the human struggle with a ray of light. A light that spreads into the illumination of the image of God inherent in humankind.

The birth of the Christ is the Eucatastrophe of the cosmos, the inconceivable grace, and the joy of Christmas.

---

[1] Tolkien, J. R. R. (1981, October 3). *The Letters of J.R.R. Tolkien*. Allen & Unwin. "Letter 88" Letter "89"

[2] Tolkien, J. R. R. (2022, October 3). *Tree and Leaf: Including 'Mythopoeia* (International Edition). HarperCollins Publishers Ltd.

LECTIO DIVINA

Take a moment to breathe deeply. Close your eyes and invite Holy Spirit to speak to you as you read God's Word. Your invitation can be as simple as, "God, I recognize that in this moment, as in all moments, I am in your presence. Speak for your servant is listening."

READ:

But the angel said to them, "Do not be afraid. I bring you good news that will cause great joy for all the people. 11 Today in the town of David a Savior has been born to you; he is the Messiah, the Lord. Luke 2:10-11 [NIV]

Take a moment to allow the Scripture to sink in. Now, go back and read it two more times. Each time, read slowly and pay special attention to any word or phrase that sticks out to you.

Ask Holy Spirit to reveal to you why (if any) word or phrase stuck out during your reading. Use the space below to journal your thoughts.

_____

_____

_____

_____

_____

_____

_____

WEEK 3: DAY THREE

In the beginning was the Word, and the Word was with God, and the Word was God. 2 He was with God in the beginning. 3 Through him all things were made; without him nothing was made that has been made. 4 In him was life, and that life was the light of all mankind. 5 The light shines in the darkness, and the darkness has not overcome it,... 9 The true light that gives light to everyone was coming into the world.... 12 Yet to all who did receive him, to those who believed in his name, he gave the right to become children of God. John 1:1-5, 9, 12 [NIV]

***

For as long as I can remember, the first chapter of the Gospel of John has captivated me with its beauty and wonder. It is my favorite passage to meditate on during Advent as it masterfully retells the creation narrative of Genesis through the lens of Christ.

What I love most about this passage is how John describes Christ, not first by how He comes into the world, but rather as He was before coming into the world.

In the beginning (Genesis 1:1) was the Word. He has been ever-present. Unceasing. Steadfast since before creation.

The Word was with God, and the Word was God. He was in community with God and possessed the authority of God.

Through the power of the Word, all things were made, visible and invisible, in heaven and on earth (Col 1:16). In the beginning, God spoke (Genesis 1:3), thereby unleashing the power of Christ to bring creation into existence.

In the Word was life, and that life was the light of all mankind. This light shines in the darkness, and the darkness has not overcome it (Genesis 1:4).

This is the portrait of power and might John paints to introduce us to the Messiah.

What strikes me most is the contrast between who He was and how He arrived. Here is the very being by which the cosmos was created and is held together, and He chooses to come not in power but humbly.

The One who was the creative force behind the breath of God that brings life now lies in a cave gasping for oxygen as He uses breath in his lungs for the first time.

The Word by which all living beings are dependent for life is now reliant on His mother for nourishment and protection.

The Light that shines on everyone, regardless of race, gender, or socioeconomic status, now lies in a manger in the dark because His family was turned away from the lights at the inn.

The King of Kings (1 Tim 6:15) has come as a child to make way for those who receive Him to become children of God.

Here exists the Christ child who is the Word.

LECTIO DIVINA

Take a moment to breathe deeply. Close your eyes and invite Holy Spirit to speak to you as you read God's Word. Your invitation can be as simple as, "God, I recognize that in this moment, as in all moments, I am in your presence. Speak for your servant is listening."

READ:

In the beginning was the Word, and the Word was with God, and the Word was God. 2 He was with God in the beginning. 3 Through him all things were made; without him nothing was made that has been made. 4 In him was life, and that life was the light of all mankind. 5 The light shines in the darkness, and the darkness has not overcome it,... 9 The true light that gives light to everyone was coming into the world.... 12 Yet to all who did receive him, to those who believed in his name, he gave the right to become children of God. John 1:1-5, 9, 12 [NIV]

Take a moment to allow the Scripture to sink in. Now, go back and read it two more times. Each time, read slowly and pay special attention to any word or phrase that sticks out to you.

Ask Holy Spirit to reveal to you why (if any) word or phrase stuck out during your reading. Use the space below to journal your thoughts.

_____

_____

_____

_____

_____

_____

WEEK 3: DAY FOUR

The Word became flesh and made his dwelling (skēnoō) among us. We have seen his glory, the glory of the one and only Son, who came from the Father, full of grace and truth. John 1:14 [NIV]

***

The Tabernacle was the place where God's presence and glory (Exodus 40) dwelt with Israel. Because Israel had not settled in the Promised Land, they were forced to roam in the wilderness. This was problematic for many reasons, not least of which was it prevented them from building a permanent place for God to dwell among them.

For those of us who live on this side of the covenant promise of God, that may not seem like a big deal. After all, if God is omnipresent, then He is always with us. Why would anyone need a specific place to meet with God?

Perhaps I can use the desire many have for marriage to explain the desire for God to dwell in a special way with His people.

I married my wife because I had a deep desire to share the entirety of my remaining life with her. It wasn't enough for me to be able to meet her at different places around town. I wanted to live life with her. I wanted her to be the first person I see when I woke up and the last one I see before falling asleep. I wanted to dwell with her in a way that is unlike anyone else in my life.

It is the way in which I am present in her life, and she is present in mine, that makes our marriage different from other relationships in my life. We live and dwell together.

For Israel, the means by which they, and the rest of the world, would know that YHWH was their God was by how He dwelt among them in a way that was different than His presence in the world (Exodus 29:45-46). This idea was symbolically represented by the Tabernacle.

Just like Israel was being forced to live in tents, God Himself would dwell in His own tent (tabernacle) among His people.

The Tabernacle and Israel's wandering in the desert was such an essential piece of Israel's history that God commanded them to observe a special holiday called Sukkot (Lev 23:34-43), also called the Feast of Tabernacles, to commemorate it throughout their generations.

Enter John 1:14. John says that the Word became flesh and dwelt among us. The Greek word the NIV translates as dwelt is *skēnoō,* and it means to "live in a tent." [1]

John points to the time in Israel's history when God dwelt, temporarily, among His people. John is setting Jesus up to be the human embodiment of what the Tabernacle pointed toward: the presence of God dwelling with His people.

God's presence had returned to His people. The joy of which newlyweds have tasted. He would dwell with them in a special way.

This temporary Tabernacle would not be present forever (John 16:7). Instead, it would make a way for all who call upon Him to become Temples of God themselves (1 Cor 3:16-17).

---

[1] [BibleProject]. (2021, November 2). *John 1 – The Word Becomes Human* [Video]. YouTube. Retrieved October 4, 2022, from https://www.youtube.com/watch?v=XgslCbXOOIE

LECTIO DIVINA

Take a moment to breathe deeply. Close your eyes and invite Holy Spirit to speak to you as you read God's Word. Your invitation can be as simple as, "God, I recognize that in this moment, as in all moments, I am in your presence. Speak for your servant is listening."

READ:

The Word became flesh and made his dwelling among us. We have seen his glory, the glory of the one and only Son, who came from the Father, full of grace and truth. John 1:14 [NIV]

Take a moment to allow the Scripture to sink in. Now, go back and read it two more times. Each time, read slowly and pay special attention to any word or phrase that sticks out to you.

Ask Holy Spirit to reveal to you why (if any) word or phrase stuck out during your reading. Use the space below to journal your thoughts.

_____

_____

_____

_____

_____

_____

_____

_____

WEEK 3: DAY FIVE

Surely God is my salvation; I will trust and not be afraid. The LORD, the LORD himself, is my strength and my defense; he has become my salvation." 3 **With joy you will draw water from the wells of salvation.** 4 In that day you will say: "Give praise to the LORD, proclaim his name; make known among the nations what he has done, and proclaim that his name is exalted. 5 Sing to the LORD, for he has done glorious things; let this be known to all the world. 6 Shout aloud and sing for joy, people of Zion, for great is the Holy One of Israel among you." Isaiah 12:2-6 [NIV]

***

Ancient wells were an integral piece of daily life. In many ways, they were the source of life because they provided water for nourishment and cleansing for yourself and your community.

While the need for wells in most western settings has been replaced by modern technologies, the symbolism of wells is still relevant and powerful.

We all have symbolic wells we head to regularly. For some, it's careers. For others, it's family. We rush to friends, material possessions, sports, or books, hoping to draw life and sustenance out of them.

The danger is that those wells can and will run dry. And when dry wells are your only source of life, your life dries up with them. It's why you can't live off of the feelings your family gives you. It's why you won't ever find ultimate purpose and fulfillment in your career, no matter how high you climb. It's why no sensation, rush, or pleasure ever lasts beyond mere moments.

If you constantly seek life from dry wells, you'll end up exhausted. You'll be frustrated by their lack of ability to sustain you. You'll be left confused and bewildered at how a well that once brought you such joy, and peace, now leaves you feeling desperate and depressed.

There is only one well that never runs dry: the well of the LORD's salvation.

In Isaiah 11, the prophet writes about the coming Messiah who will have "The Spirit of the LORD resting on Him" and says He will "raise a banner for the nations and gather the exiles of Israel."

According to Isaiah, when Messiah comes, the people of God will be able to draw joyfully from the well of salvation because the LORD will be their strength and defense.

Where other wells have failed to sustain us, this well will give unending life because "the LORD has become my salvation."

This makes this particular well distinct from any other well in one's life. Other wells run dry because they are transient and weak, unlike the LORD, who "is the everlasting God" that does "not grow tired or weary."

This well brings not only the life and freedom that comes with salvation through God's grace and mercy but true joy.

It is a joy from knowing that your life is safely wrapped up in the victory Jesus won for you.

This victory is an unending source of life and peace because the LORD has become your strength and defender.

LECTIO DIVINA

Take a moment to breathe deeply. Close your eyes and invite Holy Spirit to speak to you as you read God's Word. Your invitation can be as simple as, "God, I recognize that in this moment, as in all moments, I am in your presence. Speak for your servant is listening."

READ:

Surely God is my salvation; I will trust and not be afraid. The LORD, the LORD himself, is my strength and my defense; he has become my salvation." 3 **With joy you will draw water from the wells of salvation.** 4 In that day you will say: "Give praise to the LORD, proclaim his name; make known among the nations what he has done, and proclaim that his name is exalted. 5 Sing to the LORD, for he has done glorious things; let this be known to all the world. 6 Shout aloud and sing for joy, people of Zion, for great is the Holy One of Israel among you." Isaiah 12:2-6 [NIV]

Take a moment to allow the Scripture to sink in. Now, go back and read it two more times. Each time, read slowly and pay special attention to any word or phrase that sticks out to you.

Ask Holy Spirit to reveal to you why (if any) word or phrase stuck out during your reading. Use the space below to journal your thoughts.

_____

_____

_____

_____

_____

_____

WEEK 3: DAY SIX

And there were shepherds living out in the fields nearby, keeping watch over their flocks at night. 9 An angel of the Lord appeared to them, and the glory of the Lord shone around them, and they were terrified. 10 But the angel said to them, "Do not be afraid. **I bring you good news that will cause great joy for all the people.** 11 Today in the town of David a Savior has been born to you; he is the Messiah, the Lord. Luke 2:8-11 [NIV]

***

During this period in history, most "good religious" people would have despised shepherds. Shepherds didn't keep the details of the ceremonial laws since they were always in the fields tending their flocks. Their responsibilities to their flock also meant they weren't often around other people. One can imagine how this would affect your understanding of what's socially acceptable and, thereby, your social status.

This is why the angel bringing the message of Messiah to the shepherds is so fascinating. Their culture thought of them as uncivilized, unholy people. And while God's people didn't think much of them, God chose them to be the first to receive the message of the birth of the Christ child.

As is often the case, God seems especially concerned with the disenfranchised. He welcomes the ones whom society has rejected by inviting them into His activity in the world. He reaches out to the individuals whom "holy people" have dubbed unclean, and then He chooses them to be the recipients of the greatest message the world has ever received. God sends them a message that will cause great joy, not just for the elite or the rejected, but for all people.

71

One of my favorite Christmas songs as a child was "Santa Claus is Coming to Town." [1] It's a great and festive song filled with awful theology. [2] I didn't realize how much that song had shaped my view of Christmas and Christianity until a few years ago.

The subtle idea I picked up from the song was that Christmas is only for the "nice" people. The ones who are good and clean. The civilized. The holy.

Subconsciously, I had subscribed to the idea that naughty people didn't deserve to celebrate Christmas. They didn't make the celebration list because *he* checked. Twice. There was no room at the party for anyone who didn't make the nice list.

Living under this belief meant that my joy and peace were tied directly to my performance, whether or not I thought I was on the holy list that year. Had I done enough to earn God's favor? Had I made too many mistakes, and now my sins had canceled out whatever small amount of good I had done? If other people had rejected me, surely it was for a good reason. They knew something I didn't, and their rejection proved that I didn't make the nice list.

What freed me from that false belief was the story of God choosing the shepherds to be the first recipients and deliverers of the good news of great joy. God used the people that weren't on their culture's nice list to show that joy had come for everyone.

Christmas has to be good news for all people; otherwise, it can't bring joy to the world. It's good news for shepherds. It's good news for pastors. It's good news for doctors, prostitutes, sinners, and saints. Because we all need rescuing.

---

[1] Wikipedia contributors. (2022, October 13). Santa Claus Is Comin' to Town. Wikipedia. Retrieved October 14, 2022, from https://en.wikipedia.org/wiki/Santa_Claus_Is_Comin'_to_Town

[2] I, of course do not blame Haven Gillepsie for this poor theology. I'm sure he did not intend to write a theological discourse with this song. It was my own misunderstanding of who God is, and what He intends to do in the world, that resulted in my incorrect belief.

LECTIO DIVINA

Take a moment to breathe deeply. Close your eyes and invite Holy Spirit to speak to you as you read God's Word. Your invitation can be as simple as, "God, I recognize that in this moment, as in all moments, I am in your presence. Speak for your servant is listening."

READ:

And there were shepherds living out in the fields nearby, keeping watch over their flocks at night. 9 An angel of the Lord appeared to them, and the glory of the Lord shone around them, and they were terrified. 10 But the angel said to them, "Do not be afraid. **I bring you good news that will cause great joy for all the people.** 11 Today in the town of David a Savior has been born to you; he is the Messiah, the Lord. Luke 2:8-11 [NIV]

Take a moment to allow the Scriptures to sink in. Now, go back and read them two more times. Each time, read slowly and pay special attention to any word or phrase that sticks out to you.

Ask Holy Spirit to reveal to you why (if any) word or phrase stuck out during your reading. Use the space below to journal your thoughts.

_____

_____

_____

_____

_____

_____

WEEK 3: DAY SEVEN

for you know very well that the day of the Lord will come like a thief in the night. 3 While people are saying, "Peace and safety," destruction will come on them suddenly, as labor pains on a pregnant woman, and they will not escape. 4 But you, brothers and sisters, are not in darkness so that this day should surprise you like a thief. 5 You are all children of the light and children of the day. We do not belong to the night or to the darkness. 1 Thessalonians 5:2-5 [NIV]

"Let all mortal flesh keep silence, and with fear and trembling stand; Ponder nothing earthly minded, for with blessing in his hand Christ our God to earth descended, our full homage to demand. Rank on rank the host of heaven spreads its vanguard on the way, As the light of light descending from the realm of endless day, That the powers of hell may vanish as the darkness clears away. At his feet the six-winged seraph; cherubim with sleepless eye, Veil their faces to the Presence, as with ceaseless voice they cry, "Alleluia, Alleluia! Alleluia, Lord Most High!"
-Liturgy of St. James [1]

***

Dietrich Bonhoeffer once said, "The coming of God is truly not only a joyous message, but is, first, frightful news for anyone who has a conscience." [2]

While this may feel like a strange sentiment during Christmas, it is prevalent in the Jewish scriptures and was shared by many early church mothers and fathers.

God is holy (Lev 11:44), and when Christ returns, He will cast judgment on those who have done evil. We like to focus on the love of God and the grace Jesus brings to those who accept Him

---

[1] Wikipedia contributors. (2022a, August 31). Liturgy of Saint James. Wikipedia. Retrieved October 18, 2022, from https://en.wikipedia.org/wiki/Liturgy_of_Saint_James

[2] Bonhoeffer, D., Riess, J., & Dean, O. C., Jr. (2010, August 30). *God Is in the Manger: Reflections on Advent and Christmas* (7/31/10 ed.). Westminster John Knox Press.

as Lord, particularly during Christmas. But what power has love if it does not express itself in accepting the faults of the one it loves? How sweet can grace be if it isn't entirely undeserving?

For example, the potency of my wife's love for me isn't found in the enjoyment she experiences in being with me during my brightest moments but in her choice to remain wholly present with me in my darkest moments. That is the power of love—it carries with it the acknowledgment that my dark moments are ugly and undeserving of her love.

What power has grace if it does not manifest itself as covering the inexcusable sins of its object? The potency of my wife's grace in forgiving the sins I have committed against her lies not in sins that could be chalked up as mere mistakes. Rather her grace shines brightest against the sins I committed that deserve judgment and penalty.

Contrast the relationship of a spouse with that of a holy, righteous God. Sin and evil cannot stand in the presence of God any more than a block of ice can rest on the sun. This reality does not make the sun out to be filled with anger and malice because the ice melts in its presence. Rather, the ice melting happens due to the sun being what it is.

This is why many church fathers and mothers had a healthy fear of the day of the LORD. This fear of judgment stems from a realization that we deserve to be judged because of how we actively worked against the kingdom of God through our evil acts. None of us can stand in God's presence without the grace and love brought to us in and through Christ.

We would be consumed by God's holiness if we did not have the covering of the Babe in the Manger. This revelation causes joy to well up inside, not because we didn't once live in the darkness but because we no longer belong to it. This is the joyous message that comes to life after the fright of grasping one's own sinfulness.

LECTIO DIVINA

Take a moment to breathe deeply. Close your eyes and invite Holy Spirit to speak to you as you read God's Word. Your invitation can be as simple as, "God, I recognize that in this moment, as in all moments, I am in your presence. Speak for your servant is listening."

READ:
for you know very well that the day of the Lord will come like a thief in the night. 3 While people are saying, "Peace and safety," destruction will come on them suddenly, as labor pains on a pregnant woman, and they will not escape. 4 But you, brothers and sisters, are not in darkness so that this day should surprise you like a thief. 5 You are all children of the light and children of the day. We do not belong to the night or to the darkness. 1 Thessalonians 5:2-5 [NIV]

Take a moment to allow the Scriptures to sink in. Now, go back and read each two more times. Each time, read slowly and pay special attention to any word or phrase that sticks out to you.

Ask Holy Spirit to reveal to you why (if any) word or phrase stuck out during your reading. Use the space below to journal your thoughts.

_____

_____

_____

_____

_____

_____

L O V E

"And then, just when everything is bearing down on us to such an extent that we can scarcely withstand it, the Christmas message comes to tell us that all our ideas are wrong, and that what we take to be evil and dark is really good and light because it comes from God.

"Our eyes are at fault, that is all. God is in the manger, wealth in poverty, light in darkness, succor in abandonment. No evil can befall us; whatever men may do to us, they cannot but serve the God who is secretly revealed as love and rules the world and our lives."[1]

Dietrich Bonhoeffer

---

[1] Bonhoeffer, Dietrich. God Is in the Manger (p. 5). Presbyterian Publishing Corporation. Kindle Edition.

WEEK 4: DAY ONE

The LORD your God is with you, the Mighty Warrior who saves. **He will take great delight in you; in his love he will no longer rebuke you, but will rejoice over you with singing."** 18 "I will remove from you all who mourn over the loss of your appointed festivals, which is a burden and reproach for you. 19 At that time I will deal with all who oppressed you. I will rescue the lame; I will gather the exiles. I will give them praise and honor in every land where they have suffered shame. Zephaniah 3:17-19 [NIV]

***

The prophet Zephaniah describes what Messiah will do when he arrives by declaring that He will "take great delight in you; in his love he will no longer rebuke you, but will rejoice over you with singing."

The thought of Jesus singing over me makes me quite uncomfortable. I could blame it on my modern, western concept of masculinity or on the fact that it's utterly foreign to my experience in life.

And while those things are at play, the truth is that's not why the idea makes me uncomfortable.

It's because I don't fully believe I'm worthy of it.

Who am I to elicit a response like that from the Son of God? Why should someone like me receive such an intimate act from the King of Kings?

It's easy for me to get caught up in my mistakes. The things I've failed to do. The people I've hurt and the time I've wasted. All these things left unchecked produce in me a spirit of condemnation. This is not what Jesus came to do.

Messiah came to save, not to condemn (Romans 8:1). He came to calm us with his love (Zephaniah 3:17), not to shame us into being better versions of ourselves. He came to comfort us when we mourn (Matthew 5:4). He came to heal our sickness (Isaiah 53:5).

And He came to rejoice and sing over us with gladness. This rejoicing comes not because of how well we have excelled in life or because of the moral standard we live by. It comes because of His love for us.

The unconditional love of God is a difficult concept to grasp because most of us have only caught short glimpses of this type of love from others. The saying, "I'll always love you," never quite held true. We made mistakes, lashed out, failed, and the love of another was withdrawn.

Zephaniah uses language that would typically describe two lovers with a deep level of intimacy. He's painting a picture of enraptured love in this text to describe what it will be like when Messiah comes. This is no accident. The prophet is trying to tap into this desire we all have to be fully known by another and still, with all of our faults and inconsistencies in view, be wholly loved. So much so that it causes our lover to sing over us.

The reason Christmas is full of such wonder and awe thousands of years later is because somewhere inside every person is this deep, deep desire to hear the song once more.

Like children who beg their parents to do it again, we cannot get enough of the divine declaration that says we matter. We want to experience again the heavens parting and our beloved coming for us amid death, evil, and decay.

We want to know that the song is not over, no matter what has transpired over the last year.

We want to believe we are loved.

Because we are.

LECTIO DIVINA

Take a moment to breathe deeply. Close your eyes and invite Holy Spirit to speak to you as you read God's Word. Your invitation can be as simple as, "God, I recognize that in this moment, as in all moments, I am in your presence. Speak for your servant is listening."

READ:

The LORD your God is with you, the Mighty Warrior who saves. **He will take great delight in you; in his love he will no longer rebuke you, but will rejoice over you with singing."** 18 "I will remove from you all who mourn over the loss of your appointed festivals, which is a burden and reproach for you. 19 At that time I will deal with all who oppressed you. I will rescue the lame; I will gather the exiles. I will give them praise and honor in every land where they have suffered shame.
Zephaniah 3:17-19 [NIV]

Take a moment to allow the Scripture to sink in. Now, go back and read it two more times. Each time, read slowly and pay special attention to any word or phrase that sticks out to you.

Ask Holy Spirit to reveal to you why (if any) word or phrase stuck out during your reading. Use the space below to journal your thoughts.

_____

_____

_____

_____

_____

_____

WEEK 4: DAY TWO

Therefore the Lord himself will give you a sign: The virgin will conceive and give birth to a son, and will call him Immanuel. Isaiah 7:14 [NIV]

The Word became flesh and made his dwelling among us. We have seen his glory, the glory of the one and only Son, who came from the Father, full of grace and truth. John 1:14 [NIV]

***

Anyone who has ever loved will tell you that the heart's chief desire is to be present with the beloved. It doesn't matter whether or not it is romantic love, familial love, or the love shared between friends.

All these types of love share a common desire to be with the one they love. Their heart will ache if too much time passes without them being able to spend quality time with their beloved.

The human capacity for love, and the longing that love brings, all find their origin in God, who is love (1 John 4:8). From the beginning, God wanted to be present with His creation like any lover wants to be present with the one whom they love.

One of the first pictures of God we're given in Genesis is Him walking through the Garden of Eden, presumably searching for Adam and Eve so that He could spend time with them in the cool breeze of the evening. God was not walking around in the Garden like a sentry on patrol. God was in the Garden so He could spend time and be present with His people.

It is only after Adam and Eve are separated from God by sin that the interactions between God and mankind become distant, and primarily through a mediator like Moses or the High Priests. This distance is introduced, not as a punishment or because God is angry. It's a layer of protection, so that sinful people are not consumed by God's holiness (Deuteronomy 4:23-25).

Isaiah says that when Messiah arrives, He will be called Immanuel, which means "God with us" or "with us is God." The prophet is simultaneously pointing backward to the Garden and God's original presence with humanity while also pointing forward to the day when God's presence will be present with humankind again.

This prophecy comes not just for our own good but from God's desire to be with His people.

We so easily forget that it is not just us who crave to be in God's presence; God also yearns to be with us. The driving force behind Christ's coming into the world was love (1 John 4:9). God the Father had a deep, deep longing to be reunited with His creation because of His love for us.

The first Christmas wasn't simply about a birth. It's the pivotal moment when two lovers are finally reunited. Like a parent embracing their child after many sleepless nights spent apart, God's presence had returned to wrap His arms around His people.

And this time, God being present was entirely unlike the glimpses Israel had of His presence throughout its history, like pillars of fire, or smoke rising from The Temple.

This time, God returned as He was before sin separated Him from His beloved. Though His form was different, He was now present in the cool breeze of the evening, living and breathing among His people under the stars of Bethlehem.

The love of the Creator had been born, and with the first few cries from His lungs, He declared, "with us is God."

LECTIO DIVINA

Take a moment to breathe deeply. Close your eyes and invite Holy Spirit to speak to you as you read God's Word. Your invitation can be as simple as, "God, I recognize that in this moment, as in all moments, I am in your presence. Speak for your servant is listening."

READ:
The wolf will live with the lamb, the leopard will lie down with the goat, the calf and the lion and the yearling together; and a little child will lead them. 7 The cow will feed with the bear, their young will lie down together, and the lion will eat straw like the ox. 8 The infant will play near the cobra's den, and the young child will put its hand into the viper's nest. 9 They will neither harm nor destroy on all my holy mountain, for the earth will be filled with the knowledge of the LORD as the waters cover the sea.
Isaiah 11:6-9 [NIV]

Take a moment to allow the Scripture to sink in. Now, go back and read it two more times. Each time, read slowly and pay special attention to any word or phrase that sticks out to you.

Ask Holy Spirit to reveal to you why (if any) word or phrase stuck out during your reading. Use the space below to journal your thoughts.

_____

_____

_____

_____

_____

_____

WEEK 4: DAY THREE

He gives strength to the weary and increases the power of the weak. Isaiah 40:29 [NIV]

"That ... is the unrecognized mystery of this world: Jesus Christ. That this Jesus of Nazareth, the carpenter, was Himself the Lord of glory: that was the mystery of God. It was a mystery because God became poor, low, lowly, and weak out of love for humankind, because God became a human being like us, so that we would become divine, and because He came to us so that we would come to him."[1] Dietrich Bonhoeffer

***

The Christmas story has power only for those aware of their lowliness. Kings and rulers have tried to suppress the story from the first moment it was unleashed into the world as it does not fit with their methods of conquering, violence, and subjection to gain power.

Herod was the first to try, and he found, as all others who came after him, that the divine narrative cannot be thwarted by the carnal weapons those in power are bound to use.

The story puzzles those in power because it runs counter to our own fallen nature that seeks revenge for wrongs done. The people of God had rejected Him over and over and over again. They (we) had chosen to abuse creation rather than be with the Creator. They (we) left the divine feast of presence to lie in the mud, drink salt water, and feast on feces, all the while inviting others to follow our lead.

And yet, even though God had every reason to subject

---

[1] Bonhoeffer, Dietrich. God Is in the Manger (p. 23). Presbyterian Publishing Corporation. Kindle Edition.

humanity to punishment and wrath, He doesn't.

Humanity had fallen as low as we could. And rather than push us away because of our lowliness, God enters it with us. The God of the universe becomes the Babe in the Manger. The Cosmic Christ becomes the Christ Child. The eternal Word becomes fragile flesh. The God of the universe enters our manufactured mud pit.

This is the mystery of the Christmas story. How could God, who is perfection, enter into the messy, confused, broken story of a people who had rejected Him? Perhaps the answer is, how could God, who is perfection, not enter into the messy, confused, broken story of a people who had rejected Him?

God had shared His outline from the very beginning. He always chose broken, humble people to work His miracles throughout history. Only we didn't notice. We assumed He worked through the best of the best, as we often choose. Perhaps this is why we whitewash characters in the Scriptures and turn them into Bible Heroes rather than allow them to be deeply flawed people in the hands of a perfect God.

That first Christmas night, Christ enters the messy, confused, broken story of humanity not as a conquering ruler but as a helpless child. Rather than rule from on high, God chooses the weakest, most vulnerable human state possible to begin His rule among His people. He does this to show, once again, that the Kingdom of Heaven is not bound to the same carnal weapons as earthly kingdoms.

The Kingdom of Heaven's power comes from grace which does the costly thing when it's unmerited. Mercy which does the helpful thing when it's unwarranted. Faith which holds fast when logic says give up. And love which is present even after rejection.

This is why the power of the Christmas story is available only to those aware of their lowliness. Because it was in our lowly state that Christ joined us, and He asks us to go and do likewise.

LECTIO DIVINA

Take a moment to breathe deeply. Close your eyes and invite Holy Spirit to speak to you as you read God's Word. Your invitation can be as simple as, "God, I recognize that in this moment, as in all moments, I am in your presence. Speak for your servant is listening."

READ:

He gives strength to the weary and increases the power of the weak. Isaiah 40:29 [NIV]

Take a moment to allow the Scripture to sink in. Now, go back and read it two more times. Each time, read slowly and pay special attention to any word or phrase that sticks out to you.

Ask Holy Spirit to reveal to you why (if any) word or phrase stuck out during your reading. Use the space below to journal your thoughts.

_____

_____

_____

_____

_____

_____

_____

_____

WEEK 4: DAY FIVE

Out of the depths I cry to you, LORD; 2 Lord, hear my voice. Let your ears be attentive to my cry for mercy. **3 If you, LORD, kept a record of sins, Lord, who could stand? 4 But with you there is forgiveness, so that we can, with reverence, serve you.** 5 I wait for the LORD, my whole being waits, and in his word I put my hope. 6 I wait for the Lord more than watchmen wait for the morning, more than watchmen wait for the morning. **7 Israel, put your hope in the LORD, for with the LORD is unfailing love and with him is full redemption. 8 He himself will redeem Israel from all their sins.** Psalms 130:1-8 [NIV]

***

Out of our depths, we cry out for love. We long to feel the warm embrace of the Creator's love for us. The challenge for many is not found in the desire to be loved by God but in the acceptance of the love of God.

Somewhere inside us, we know that love cannot exist alongside a list of offenses. It may be because we have our own past and present list of offenses committed against us. We have felt the love we once had for another grow cold as we held tight to how they wronged us. We refused to let it go because they had not earned the right of forgiveness.

These lists we keep can and will block us from receiving God's love (Mark 11:22-26), but even the person who has burned their lists may find it difficult to accept the love of God. This stems from a lack of understanding of the true character of God.

If God is love (1 John 4:16) and love keeps no record of wrongs (1 Corinthians 13:5), then what the Psalmist claims must be true: "with the LORD is unfailing love." God loves and saves not out of obligation but out of His very essence.

God did not look at the goodness you're capable of and decide you were worth loving. When you were an enemy of God (Romans 5:8), His love snatched you out of death's grasp. His love met you at your worst, not your best.

This revelation frees us from having to perform to receive God's love. While each of us will give an account one day for how we lived on this earth (Romans 14:12), that account does not dictate God's love for us.

This is the great hope made available to all who call on the name of Jesus. With God, there is unfailing love. As long as your hope is found in God, there is no sin, past, present, or future, that is capable of causing His love for you to fail. And if no sin can remove God's love from you, what possibly could?

Who shall separate us from the love of Christ? Shall trouble, hardship, persecution, famine, nakedness, danger, or sword? As it is written: "For your sake we face death all day long; we are considered as sheep to be slaughtered." No, in all these things we are more than conquerors through him who loved us. For I am convinced that neither death nor life, neither angels nor demons, neither the present nor the future, nor any powers, neither height nor depth, nor anything else in all creation, will be able to separate us from the love of God that is in Christ Jesus our Lord. (Romans 835-39 NIV)

The only thing we must do is place our hope in the LORD and believe the record of wrong has been erased. For He, Himself has redeemed us.

LECTIO DIVINA

Take a moment to breathe deeply. Close your eyes and invite Holy Spirit to speak to you as you read God's Word. Your invitation can be as simple as, "God, I recognize that in this moment, as in all moments, I am in your presence. Speak for your servant is listening."

READ:

Out of the depths I cry to you, LORD; 2 Lord, hear my voice. Let your ears be attentive to my cry for mercy. **3 If you, LORD, kept a record of sins, Lord, who could stand? 4 But with you there is forgiveness, so that we can, with reverence, serve you.** 5 I wait for the LORD, my whole being waits, and in his word I put my hope. 6 I wait for the Lord more than watchmen wait for the morning, more than watchmen wait for the morning. **7 Israel, put your hope in the LORD, for with the LORD is unfailing love and with him is full redemption. 8 He himself will redeem Israel from all their sins.** Psalms 130:1-8 [NIV]

Take a moment to allow the Scripture to sink in. Now, go back and read it two more times. Each time, read slowly and pay special attention to any word or phrase that sticks out to you.

Ask Holy Spirit to reveal to you why (if any) word or phrase stuck out during your reading. Use the space below to journal your thoughts.

_____

_____

_____

_____

_____

WEEK 4: DAY SIX

...prepare the way for the LORD; make straight in the desert a highway for our God. 4 Every valley shall be raised up, every mountain and hill made low; the rough ground shall become level, the rugged places a plain. 5 And the glory of the LORD will be revealed, and all people will see it together. Isaiah 40:3b-5 [NIV]

..."Teacher, this woman was caught in the act of adultery. 5 In the Law Moses commanded us to stone such women. Now what do you say"... 7 When they kept on questioning him, he straightened up and said to them, "Let any one of you who is without sin be the first to throw a stone at her... 9 At this, those who heard began to go away one at a time, the older ones first, until only Jesus was left, with the woman still standing there. 10 Jesus straightened up and asked her, "Woman, where are they? Has no one condemned you?" 11 "No one, sir," she said. "Then neither do I condemn you," Jesus declared. "Go now and leave your life of sin." John 8:1-11 [NIV]

***

Isaiah prophesied that Messiah would fix the world's brokenness when he came. Because of Christ's work, every valley of pride, every mountain of fear, and every hill of selfishness would be flattened. The crookedness of humanity would be made straight. The rough exterior of our world would disappear, the things that bring pain and heartache, tears and shame.

And all humankind would witness the salvation of God.

It's easy to forget why Jesus came into the world, particularly during the torrent of busyness we experience during the Christmas season. Christ came not to receive gifts from wise men nor to receive praise from shepherds. This newborn child came to fix the brokenness of our world. He came to stop terror attacks and to put an end to racism. He came to heal disease and to clean the stain of sin from our lives.

The Christ child did this, not simply by sacrificing His life for us thirty-three years later. He did it by living as an example of what it means to be God's image bearer. We often think of Jesus only as the Babe in the Manger or the Man on the Cross. But the power of Messiah came not from where He was born, nor from how He died—but from how He lived.

It was the life of Christ that gave significance to His birth and was what caused His death to be revolutionary. His life was both a revelation and a call, showing through the power of Holy Spirit how humans can cultivate love, grace, and mercy amidst evil, tyranny, and violence. His life was a call to participate in this new way to be human.

This new way of being human does not condemn people for their sins. Instead, it reflects the grace and mercy of God to the individual. After all, it is the kindness of God (Romans 2:4) that leads to repentance. This kindness does not excuse sin; it beckons others to leave their life of sin behind so that they, too, may experience the abundant life (John 10:10) of those who believe.

Jesus bending down and writing in the dust, as the woman's accusers stood with stones in hand, was an act of extreme defiance. He was straightening the crooked path the mob around him had followed religiously. What matters is not what He wrote in the dirt but the crowd's response. This leveling of the plain was something they weren't interested in. They were too committed to the old way of being human. They had found comfort in the crooked and solace in the shadows.

The one who remained got to witness the salvation of God firsthand. And with it came her own revelation and call.

Live as a new human, and make the path straight.

LECTIO DIVINA

Take a moment to breathe deeply. Close your eyes and invite Holy Spirit to speak to you as you read God's Word. Your invitation can be as simple as, "God, I recognize that in this moment, as in all moments, I am in your presence. Speak for your servant is listening."

READ:

...prepare the way for the LORD; make straight in the desert a highway for our God. 4 Every valley shall be raised up, every mountain and hill made low; the rough ground shall become level, the rugged places a plain. 5 And the glory of the LORD will be revealed, and all people will see it together. Isaiah 40:3b-5 [NIV]

At this, those who heard began to go away one at a time, the older ones first, until only Jesus was left, with the woman still standing there. 10 Jesus straightened up and asked her, "Woman, where are they? Has no one condemned you?" 11 "No one, sir," she said. "Then neither do I condemn you," Jesus declared. "Go now and leave your life of sin." John 8:9-11 [NIV]

Take a moment to allow the Scriptures to sink in. Now, go back and read them two more times. Each time, read slowly and pay special attention to any word or phrase that sticks out to you.

Ask Holy Spirit to reveal to you why (if any) word or phrase stuck out during your reading. Use the space below to journal your thoughts.

_____

_____

_____

_____

"Come, thou long expected Jesus,
Born to set your people free;
From our fears and sins release us,
Let us find our rest in thee.

Israel's strength and consolation,
Hope of all the earth thou art:
Dear desire of every nation,
Joy of every longing heart.

Born your people to deliver,
Born a child, and yet a king,
Born to reign in us for ever,

Now your gracious kingdom bring.
By your own eternal spirit
Rule in all our hearts alone;
By your all sufficient merit
Raise us to your glorious throne."[1]

-Charles Wesley

---

[1] Wikipedia contributors. (2022a, March 1). *Come, Thou Long Expected Jesus*. Wikipedia. https://en.wikipedia.org/wiki/Come,_Thou_Long_Expected_Jesus

CHRISTMAS EVE

While they were there, the time came for the baby to be born, 7 and she gave birth to her firstborn, a son. She wrapped him in cloths and placed him in a manger, because there was no guest room available for them. Luke 2:6-7 [NIV]

The Word became flesh and made his dwelling among us. We have seen his glory, the glory of the one and only Son, who came from the Father, full of grace and truth. John 1:14 [NIV]

***

The night before the birth of Christ wasn't just a silent night.

It was the culmination of four hundred years of silence.

God had not spoken directly to His people since the book of Malachi four centuries earlier. And yet, though the previous nights had also been filled with silence, this silent night was unlike the others.

For it was this silent night that would welcome the day of God's Word returning to the earth. Only this time, flesh and bone was attached. Soon the sky would split as angels declared the birth of the Savior for all people. Silence would give way to joy and singing as the glory of the LORD (James 2:1) returned to His people.

For as long as I can remember, Christmas Eve has had a stillness to it. Most years, I long for Christmas Eve more than Christmas Day. Even though I have church services to attend and family gatherings, this sense of silence seems to hover over the day for me.

The atmosphere feels different. Quieter. Near silent.

While I love celebrating Christmas with those dearest to me, my soul longs for the deep breath of the Silent Night.

Maybe it's because my experience walking with God has taught me that there are more silent nights than Christmas mornings. This is not to say that God's presence is not present and available daily. After all, Jesus is Immanuel (God with us).

However, I often find that my pace in life causes me to miss out on the ways God is present with me. I have also had many seasons where I desperately sought the intervention of God's Word only to receive another silent night that left me longing for God to speak again.

Perhaps I love Christmas Eve because it reminds me that the silence of God doesn't equate to the absence of God.

Everything is dark and quiet when the curtain falls for a stage play after an act. However, behind the curtain, the director is up to something. He's setting the stage for the final act. He's preparing to introduce the audience to the climactic resolution.

The night before Christmas reminds me that the silent nights I've experienced over the last year do not mean God was absent in my life. Instead, they point toward the night before Christ's birth. They encourage me to keep the faith, believing God is present and active behind the curtain.

Christmas Eve reminds me that even when silence is all I have ever known, God can change my entire reality with one word.

Even when the last four hundred years have been one way, all it takes is one more silent night to produce a miracle.

For it is the silent nights that prepare us to rejoice in the beauty of the morning songs.

LECTIO DIVINA

Take a moment to breathe deeply. Close your eyes and invite Holy Spirit to speak to you as you read God's Word. Your invitation can be as simple as, "God, I recognize that in this moment, as in all moments, I am in your presence. Speak for your servant is listening."

READ:

The Word became flesh and made his dwelling among us. We have seen his glory, the glory of the one and only Son, who came from the Father, full of grace and truth. John 1:14 [NIV]

Take a moment to allow the Scripture to sink in. Now, go back and read it two more times. Each time, read slowly and pay special attention to any word or phrase that sticks out to you.

Ask Holy Spirit to reveal to you why (if any) word or phrase stuck out during your reading. Use the space below to journal your thoughts.

_____

_____

_____

_____

_____

_____

_____

_____

CHRISTMAS DAY

So Joseph also went up from the town of Nazareth in Galilee to Judea, to Bethlehem the town of David, because he belonged to the house and line of David. 5 He went there to register with Mary, who was pledged to be married to him and was expecting a child. 6 While they were there, the time came for the baby to be born, 7 and she gave birth to her firstborn, a son. She wrapped him in cloths and placed him in a manger, because there was no guest room available for them. Luke 2:4-7 [NIV]

***

Today we celebrate Jesus Christ entering our world.

Here is the most extraordinary love story ever told.

The bridegroom who left the perfection of the heavens in a relentless pursuit of love. The One whose creativity carved the cosmos now lay in His own created form. The Christ, the Son of God, clothed with power from on high, has laid aside His power to come humbly as a child.

When Christ was in heaven, seated on the throne with God,

He needed nothing. Now, He was wholly dependent on God, just like us. He was entirely dependent on His mother, just like we were. He was learning to breathe through His lungs for the first time, just like we had.

The Savior of humanity was now human.

Today, we must slow down.

What a tragedy it would be if our home was found guilty of the same error as the city of Bethlehem. If, on the day of Christ's birth, He discovered that we had made no room for Him.

On Christmas day, there are three things every Christian must do.

First, we must remember what Jesus did for us. We must not forget what He gave up for us. What He sacrificed for us.

Second, we must rejoice! The God of the heavens now dwells with us in our broken state. He has come to give us life to the full (John 10:10), which is cause for grand celebration.

Lastly, we must reflect on how He arrived. Jesus chose to come humbly as a babe lying in a feeding trough. He gave up the glory of the heavens to share space with common people and animals.

Today, and every day after, we must look to enter humanity's struggles as Jesus did—humbly. For it is in the humility of Christ that we find the greatest examples of strength and love.

Maranatha.

And Merry Christmas.

LECTIO DIVINA

Take a moment to breathe deeply. Close your eyes and invite Holy Spirit to speak to you as you read God's Word. Your invitation can be as simple as, "God, I recognize that in this moment, as in all moments, I am in your presence. Speak for your servant is listening."

READ:

So Joseph also went up from the town of Nazareth in Galilee to Judea, to Bethlehem the town of David, because he belonged to the house and line of David. 5 He went there to register with Mary, who was pledged to be married to him and was expecting a child. 6 While they were there, the time came for the baby to be born, 7 and she gave birth to her firstborn, a son. She wrapped him in cloths and placed him in a manger, because there was no guest room available for them. Luke 2:4-7 [NIV]

Take a moment to allow the Scriptures to sink in. Now, go back and read each two more times. Each time, read slowly and pay special attention to any word or phrase that sticks out to you.

Ask Holy Spirit to reveal to you why (if any) word or phrase stuck out during your reading. Use the space below to journal your thoughts.

_____

_____

_____

_____

_____

_____

ABOUT THE AUTHOR

Paul Grodell III is an apprentice of Jesus, a husband, and a father. He resides in Cleveland, Ohio.

CPSIA information can be obtained
at www.ICGtesting.com
Printed in the USA
BVHW072204251122
652769BV00006B/250